Mastering the Job Interview

Your Guide to Successful Business Interviews

Alexander Chernev

Kellogg School of Management
Northwestern University

Fourth Edition

Mastering the Job Interview

Fourth Edition | July 2007

ISBN-10: 0-9763061-9-0

ISBN-13: 978-0-9763061-9-1

Table of Contents

Preface

Most business interviews offer an interesting paradox: While nearly all candidates understand the importance of taking a systematic approach to business management, few apply the same systematic approach in preparing for the interview. Instead, they approach the interview process in a haphazard manner, relying primarily on their intuition to ensure a positive outcome. This approach is, in part, based on the common belief that interviews are company-specific and, hence, interview preparation should be done on a case-by-case basis. This is incorrect. While it is true that companies do employ diverse interviewing strategies, the core set of skills required for success is virtually the same across companies. Identifying these core skills will provide you with a deeper understanding of recruiters' needs and will help you develop a successful value proposition for each individual company. The goal of this book, therefore, is to outline the logic of the interview process and offer you a systematic approach to acing each individual interview.

Mastering the Job Interview offers in-depth insights on how to develop a winning interview strategy. It outlines the basic interview principles, reveals the core skill set most recruiters seek, and identifies strategies you can use to master the job interview. The discussion is complemented by an extended set of illustrations and applications identifying specific strategies on how to ace the interview process. It includes explicit résumé and interview guidelines, sample questions and answers, and strategies for the personal experience interview.

Recruiting is not only a process of finding a job; it is also a process of discovering yourself. To be successful in the interview, you should not only have a good understanding of the needs of the recruiting company, you should also know yourself. Thus, recruiting is not only about the company discovering you but also about you discovering who you are and who you want to be, both personally and professionally.

Good luck!

About the Author

Alexander Chernev is associate professor of marketing at the Kellogg School of Management, Northwestern University, where he teaches the core marketing management course to MBA students and behavioral decision theory to Ph.D. students. He holds a Ph.D. in Psychology from Sofia University and a Ph.D. in Business Administration from Duke University. Professor Chernev's research applies theories and concepts related to consumer behavior and managerial decision making to develop successful corporate branding and customer management strategies. His research has been published in leading marketing journals, and he has received numerous teaching and research awards. He serves on the editorial boards of the top research journals and has advised many companies on issues such as strategic marketing, new product development, and customer management policies. Professor Chernev has provided career advice to numerous students, many of whom are currently working for Fortune 500 companies and others who are in the process of building their own Fortune 500 companies.

The Job Interview

Your success at the interview is determined by your ability to identify a company that can best fulfill your goals and convince recruiters from that company to hire you. To achieve that, you should be able to clearly articulate your value proposition to the company and identify factors that make you the best candidate for the job. Your successful interview performance is a function of your individual characteristics – your skills, knowledge, and experience – as well as your ability to optimally market these skills, knowledge, and experience to the recruiting company.

Preparing for the interview involves three key steps: understanding what recruiters are looking for in a candidate, creating your unique value proposition, and, finally, persuading the recruiter that you fit the needs of the company. These three steps are discussed in more detail in the first chapter. The second chapter addresses some of the key issues in writing your resume. The third chapter offers a set of strategies to master the personal experience interview (also referred to as the behavioral interview). The fourth chapter offers an overview of the case interview and identifies some of the key case-interview strategies. Finally, the appendix offers an illustration of the core skills sought by companies.

—————————— Chapter One ——————————

The Big Picture

Companies seek to hire candidates who can add value to their organization. The interviewer's goal is to identify candidates whose value proposition best fits the needs of the organization and who have the highest potential to create value for the company. Hence, your success in the interview is determined by the degree to which your value proposition fits the company's needs.

A useful approach to maximize your fit with the company involves the following three steps: (1) understand the recruiter's needs; (2) position yourself in a way that demonstrates you will add value to the company and differentiates you from the other candidates; and (3) clearly communicate your value proposition. These three steps are discussed in more detail in the following sections.

What Are Companies Looking for in a Candidate?

The goal of the interview is to ensure a fit between a candidate's relevant competencies and a company's needs. Because most of the newly hired associates are likely to work on multiple projects and be faced with a diverse set of problems, recruiters tend to seek candidates with a broad set of skills such as leadership, analytical thinking, and teamwork – skills that can be applied across diverse problems and industries. Therefore, when evaluating prospective candidates, companies tend to focus on candidates' general skills and competencies rather than on their experience related to a specific industry (e.g., pharmaceuticals, automotive, or technology). Even though industry experience is clearly beneficial, it is often viewed as a complementary asset to your core skills and competencies.

What skills do most companies seek? An in-depth analysis of companies' recruiting practices reveals that most management consulting, consumer products, and technology companies seek future management-track associates with more or less the same set of core attributes. These attributes can be classified into three categories: (1) core skills, (2) knowledge, and (3) company fit. These three sets of attributes are discussed in more detail in the following sections.

Core Skills

Core skills are the key abilities that are essential across all management functions. The core skill set includes the following eight skills:

○ **Leadership.** Leadership is the talent to take on a leadership role and is reflected in the ability to seize opportunity and take action, build a team and encourage a shared vision, keep a clear focus on the ultimate goals, and show willingness to take a personal risk to achieve these goals.

○ **Analytical skills.** Analytical skills reflect the capacity for strategic thinking, abstract reasoning, dealing with ambiguity, and an intuitive feel for numbers. Analytical skills are typically evaluated on two key dimensions: logical reasoning and quantitative skills.

○ **Creativity.** In an interview context, creativity refers to the ability to come up with an original approach that offers a simple solution to a complex problem.

○ **Teamwork.** Teamwork skills reflect the ability to collaborate with other teammates, both within and across functions (e.g., within marketing and with finance, operations, and accounting).

○ **Communication skills.** Communication skills reflect the ability to express ideas clearly, accurately, and succinctly, and to effectively disseminate information. Communication skills include the following abilities: listening, public speaking, writing, discussing, negotiating, and networking.

○ **Management skills.** Management skills reflect your professional poise, as well as the ability to meet deadlines, manage multiple tasks, coordinate different projects, and perform under pressure.

○ **Capacity to learn.** Capacity to learn reflects the ability to improve one's performance and acquire new skills.

○ **Drive.** Drive refers to personal motivation for achievement, energy level, and perseverance. It reflects willingness to overcome barriers and go outside the comfort zone in order to achieve the set goals.

Companies vary in the degree to which they value the importance of the above skills. Some companies place emphasis on a subset of these skills and seek candidates who excel only on some of these dimensions (provided, of course, that they have no deficiencies on the other dimensions). In addition, different companies use different labels for the same underlying skill (e.g., innovation instead of creativity, collaboration instead of teamwork, and motivation instead of drive). Note, however, that even though companies differ in terms of the relative importance of the required skills, as well as in terms of the specific labels used to refer to these skills, the underlying skill set is essentially the same across all companies.

To illustrate, one of the key skills sought by Procter & Gamble in its recruiting efforts is the *ability to leverage resources*, which encompasses three key skills: leadership, innovation, and collaboration. In this context, leveraging resources translates to your ability to lead the company's innovation (creativity) efforts by collaborating (teamwork) with different stakeholders such as research teams, ad agencies, product development teams, and operation teams.

In the area of management consulting, McKinsey & Company is looking for candidates who demonstrate capabilities in four critical areas: problem solving (analytical skills + creativity), achieving (management skills + drive), personal impact (teamwork + communication skills), and leadership. Rather than focusing on one particular skill, McKinsey seeks well-rounded individuals with outstanding potential in each of these areas.

Knowledge

Recruiters are also often interested in your knowledge in specific areas of importance to the interviewing company. The types of knowledge most recruiters are looking for can be organized into three general categories: functional knowledge, industry knowledge, and global knowledge.

o *Functional knowledge* reflects your familiarity with a particular functional area (e.g., marketing, accounting, finance, and consulting). Functional knowledge involves understanding the basic business terminology, principles, frameworks, and theories that are essential for performing a given business function.

o *Industry knowledge* refers to your familiarity with the specifics of the industry that is of interest to the recruiting company. Industry knowledge involves understanding industry trends, the core competencies and strategic assets of the key players, as well as the dynamics of the competition and power structure.

o *Global knowledge* refers to your familiarity with the specifics of doing business in a particular country and/or geographic area. Global knowledge involves language skills, familiarity with a country-specific culture, politics, and legal system, and, on rare occasions, even connections with local government officials, business leaders, and celebrities.

Company Fit

In addition to the basic functional skills, recruiters look for certain individual characteristics that will ensure a better fit between you and the company. Factors that are likely to ensure your fit with the company can be organized into three general categories: personality fit, commitment to the company, and interest in the functional area.

- ***Personality fit.*** Personality fit reflects various aspects of your personality in relation to the company's culture (e.g., Would you be able to adapt easily to the company culture? Are you fun to work with?).

- ***Commitment to the company.*** Commitment reflects the degree to which you are really interested in the company. Needless to say, recruiters prefer candidates who have a sincere interest in their company.

- ***Interest in the functional area.*** This factor refers to your interest in the particular functional area involved (marketing, consulting, general management, research, etc.) The underlying assumption is that the greater the fit between your interests and the job requirements, the greater the likelihood that you will make a valuable contribution to the company.

Creating Your Value Proposition

Once recruiters' needs have been identified, the next step is to articulate your value proposition vis-à-vis these needs. The goal is to identify a corresponding skill that you can bring to the company for each of the key skills sought by recruiters. A four-step approach to articulating your value proposition is shown in Figure 1 and discussed in more detail below.

Figure 1. Creating Your Value Proposition

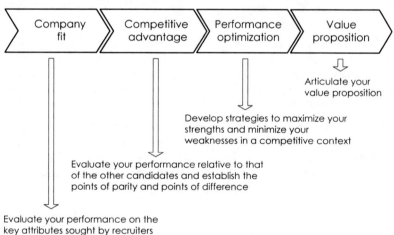

The first step is to evaluate your performance on the key attributes sought by recruiters. One simple strategy to accomplish this is to rank your performance on each attribute on a five-point scale (e.g., exceptional, above average, average, below average, poor). This will help identify areas in which you fit the company's needs, as well as areas in which you have to improve. In general, you should strive to improve in areas in which your performance is below average (or poor), as well as in areas highly valued by the company in which your performance is merely average.

The next step is to benchmark your performance relative to that of other candidates and establish the points of parity and points of difference. Because you will be compared to other candidates, it is not sufficient to be just *good*: You have to be *better* than the other candidates. One simple benchmarking method is to identify areas in which you are readily differentiated from other candidates (points of differences) and areas in which you are likely to blend in (points of parity). You can use the same five-point scale (e.g., exceptional, above average, average, below average, poor) as in the first step, but in this case your reference point is the performance of the other candidates rather than the needs of the company.

The next step is to develop strategies to optimize your performance by maximizing your strengths and minimizing your weaknesses. This is an important step, often overlooked by candidates and career counselors alike. Beware of hiding your weaknesses during the interview; this is only a temporary solution that might eventually backfire if you are not able to perform up to the standards of the company. The goal here is to improve your performance on the key attributes sought by recruiters, as well as to convert points of parity on the key attributes into points of difference. To illustrate, if you are aware that a given company emphasizes teamwork and your performance on that attribute is similar to that of the other candidates, you should consider working on improving your teamwork skills to develop a distinct advantage.

The final step is to articulate your value proposition and develop a positioning strategy. Positioning is derived by highlighting one or two aspects of your overall value proposition that most clearly communicate your value to the company and differentiate you from the other candidates. Therefore, successful positioning requires you to clearly demonstrate that your value proposition offers a better fit with the company's needs than those of the other candidates. A summary of the process of articulating your value proposition is given in the worksheet shown in Table 1.

Table 1: Positioning Worksheet

Value Proposition	Importance to the company (1=low, 5=high)	Your performance (1=low, 5=high)	Your relative performance (1=low, 5=high)
Core skills			
Leadership			
Analytical skills			
Creativity			
Teamwork			
Communication skills			
Management skills			
Capacity to learn			
Drive			
Knowledge			
Functional knowledge			
Industry knowledge			
Global knowledge			
Company fit			
Personality fit			
Commitment to the company			
Interest in the functional area			

Your unique value proposition:

Communicating Your Value Proposition

Once you understand the key value drivers for the company and articulate your unique value proposition, the next step is to develop a strategy to communicate your value proposition to the recruiting company. Communicating your value proposition starts with your résumé. The actual interview consists of several parts. It starts with an introduction, followed by questions about your personal experience and often by a case analysis. Typically, you will have an opportunity to ask questions about the company. The interview usually concludes with a closure in which you will sum up the reasons the company should hire you and establish a follow-up procedure (Figure 2). Each of these interview components is discussed in more detail below.

Figure 2. Communicating Your Value Proposition

The Interview

Your Résumé

The "perfect" résumé is the one that most clearly communicates your unique value proposition to the interviewing company. Your résumé should differentiate you from the other candidates; it should underscore your value proposition and reflect your unique experience. Do not try to emulate someone else's résumé; instead, try to communicate your own story and your own value proposition.

Contrary to popular belief, your résumé is not about what you have done in the past. It is about what you can do for the company in the future. Avoid including in your résumé facts and/or details that do not enhance your overall value to the company. Each statement on your résumé should serve the purpose of communicating to the interviewer your value proposition, thus moving a step closer to eliciting an offer. For each experience on your résumé, have a short example that demonstrates the skills important to the interviewing company (see the storyboard approach and the skills-in-context matrix in the following sections). An overview of the key résumé-writing principles is given in Chapter 2.

Introduction

Most interviews begin with an introduction in which you and the interviewer greet one another and exchange a few ice-breaking comments. It is also common for the interviewer to offer a beverage. The interview is then commonly initiated with an open-ended general question of the "tell-me-about-yourself" type – a question that also serves as the transition to the personal experience portion of the interview. Because the tell-me-about-yourself question is a quite common interview approach, it is important to master a few introductory phrases so you can start the interview by positioning yourself in a way that underscores your value to the company and differentiates you from the other candidates.

Personal Experience Interview

The personal experience interview (also referred to as a behavioral interview) aims to reveal candidates' core skills, knowledge, and their fit with the company. This part of the interview usually involves asking you to provide examples of a situation in which you demonstrated the set of skills that are important to the recruiting company. The nature of the personal experience interview and strategies for mastering it are discussed in more detail in Chapter 3 of this book.

Case Analysis

Case analysis is an integral part of many consulting, management, and marketing interviews. Case questions ask you to analyze a business problem, and your insights into the case are used to help evaluate your skills, knowledge, and fit with the company. An overview of the key issues in case analysis is offered in Chapter 4 of this book; an in-depth analysis of case interview strategies is offered in a separate book: *Mastering the Case Interview: The Complete Guide to Management, Marketing, and Strategic Consulting Case Interviews*.

Your Questions

At the end of the interview most recruiters let you ask questions. The purpose of these questions is twofold. First, they aim to provide you with additional information about the company, its current projects, culture, and work environment. Second, the questions you ask are also a part of the interview. They are used to evaluate your interest in the company, your goals, priorities, and value system.

Be prepared to ask questions about the company, its vision for the future, defining characteristics, working environment, the company's current projects, the role that newly hired associates are likely to play, prospects for growth within the company, and the likely career track. Do not ask generic questions or those for which answers could easily be found in company literature. Instead, ask questions that will help you determine if you are a good match for the position and vice versa.

Closure

Closing the interview gives you the opportunity to summarize your unique skills and reiterate your interest in the company. You can also ask whether you can provide the interviewer with any additional information and gather insights about the next step in the process (e.g., the hiring decision process and timeframe). In addition, you can ask how to contact the interviewer to follow up on the interview (e.g., by mail, email, or phone). Keep in mind that there are many ways to close the interview; your closing should fit your personality and the interviewing style of the recruiting company.

Sometimes recruiters provide you with the opportunity to close the interview by asking you a concluding question of the type "Is there anything you would like to add (anything else we should know about you)"? You can answer this question the same way you would answer the question "Why should we hire you?" Describe the key assets and competencies that you bring to the firm. You can organize them around the three key factors: skills, knowledge, and fit with the company. This can serve as a natural closure of the interview.

Follow-up

Many recruiters view the post-interview follow-up as an important part of the process. As a result, even though follow-up activity does not guarantee that you will secure the position, if done well it could enhance your chances. In general, the goal of the follow-up is threefold: (1) thank the interviewer for his/her time and the opportunity to interview for the position, (2) reiterate your interest in the company and the position, and (3) reinforce your unique value proposition to the company. In this context, the follow-up can be an important component of communicating your value proposition to the company.

A common practice is to follow up on the interview within 24 hours, either with a thank-you letter or email. The course and the outcome of the interview should help you determine the best follow-up strategy, the content of your message, and the method of communicating it.

General Interview Guidelines

Following are a number of simple rules you need to follow before, during, and after the interview to maximize your chances for success.

▸ **Before the Interview**

o Research the industry and the company. Learn more about the company's vision, value system, management, product lines, and strategic challenges.

o Find out how the company conducts its interviews. Boston Consulting Group and McKinsey, for example, provide detailed personal interview advice and case analysis examples on their websites.

o Identify the reasons you would like to work for each and every company on your list. This is a question to which you should know the answer, not only because it is likely to come up in the interview, but also because it will help you articulate your level of interest in the company.

o Identify your value to the interviewing company. What is your value proposition, that is, what are the competencies and assets you bring to the company? How would you position yourself? What makes you more valuable than other candidates interviewing for the same position?

o Be fluent with your own résumé; anticipate the likely questions and have an answer ready.

o Be prepared to ask questions about the company, such as working environment, the role that newly hired associates are likely to play, and the potential career track.

o Practice. Do mock interviews with friends, teammates, and your school's career office; videotape your interviews and get feedback; observe others' mock interviews as well.

▸ **During the Interview**

o Always have your résumé with you, even if you expect the recruiter to have a copy.

o Your attire should fit the image of the company with which you are interviewing. The more formal and/or conservative the company, the more formally and conservatively you should dress, and vice versa. If in doubt, err on the side of being more formal/conservative. You should feel comfortable in your outfit (if you cannot feel comfortable in an outfit that fits the company's image, you probably should not interview with that company).

o Make good eye contact. This will help you engage the interviewer, establish rapport, and contribute to the interactivity of the interview.

- Be a good listener. Do not interrupt the interviewer when he/she is speaking. Be prepared to take notes.

- Be positive and avoid talking about the negatives. Instead, discuss what you've learned from difficult situations and how you have overcome challenges.

- Do not get personal. In most cases, it is a good idea to stay away from topics such as the interviewer's family, physical appearance, religious or political beliefs, age and ethnic background.

- Control your nervousness. Discover where your nervous energy goes (e.g., laughing, playing with your pen, tapping your fingers), and try to channel this energy into listening and responding to the interviewer's questions and comments.

- Do not ramble. Articulate your thoughts clearly and succinctly throughout the interview.

- Project confidence and be calm even if something goes "wrong" such as a ringing cell phone during the interview or mispronouncing the name of the interviewer. Do not be thrown off track by such mistakes; keep composure, recognize the mistake, apologize if appropriate, and move on with the interview.

- Monitor your body language. Crossed arms (considered to be defensive); tapping your feet, playing with your hair, fidgeting (an indication of nervousness or boredom); and lack of eye contact are commonly viewed as negative signs. In contrast, leaning forward and nodding while listening are usually viewed as positive signs.

- Avoid using clichés. Do not simply label yourself as "analytic," "creative," and "team-player" – these concepts are very generic and not very informative. Instead, identify specific instances that vividly demonstrate your particular skills. Tell your story, not a cliché. A vivid story has a greater chance of creating a positive and lasting impression that will allow the interviewer to later link your story to your name and skills.

- Avoid discussing salary during the early rounds of the interview. While the issue of compensation can be brought up by the recruiter at any point in the interview, in most cases you should not bring up this issue without an indication from the recruiter of their willingness to make you an offer.

- Most important – relax, try to be yourself and have fun during the interview. John W. Thompson, who, while in college, worked part time selling component stereo systems and later became the CEO of the software giant Symantec, when interviewing for a sales job with IBM ended up selling a stereo system to the interviewer.

▶ **After the Interview**

○ A thank-you note (letter or email) can make a difference. Send it within a day of the interview and try to make it personal. If you send notes to more than one person from the same company, expect that the notes will be shared and try to make them sound different.

○ When feasible, collect feedback on your performance and use this feedback to improve for the next interview. Think about what worked and what did not. Identify areas for improvement and get additional practice in these areas.

Chapter Two

The Résumé

The first impression you make on the recruiting company is created by your résumé. It is your résumé that gets you to the first round of interviews. Therefore, developing an impactful résumé is a key aspect of preparing for the job interview.

Overview

Writing a résumé is often confused with the process of identifying your value proposition to recruiters. This confusion stems from the fact that writing a résumé implies that you have a clearly defined positioning strategy that underscores your unique value proposition. Writing a résumé and positioning, however, are two fundamentally different activities. Positioning outlines your unique value proposition, whereas your résumé communicates your positioning to recruiters.

The key principle in developing a résumé is that it should not simply reflect your achievements to date. To ensure your success in the recruitment process, your résumé should go beyond offering a chronological list of your achievements and clearly indicate to the recruiter how these achievements enhance your potential to create value for the company. Therefore, each line on your résumé should not only offer information about a particular experience, but should give the interviewer a reason to hire you. This is the key to the successful résumé.

Structuring the Résumé

From a structural standpoint, most résumés are organized around three main categories: *education, work experience*, and *additional information*. These three résumé components are discussed below.

Education

The education section of your résumé provides details of graduate work and college education. It typically includes your degree subject, university, GPA, and any major distinctions (e.g., Magna cum laude), awards, and prizes that might help document your academic abilities. When describing your academic experiences, it is important to explain an accomplishment if you think the recruiter might not understand its importance (e.g., top 1% of students nationally). You might also include any significant academic accomplishments (e.g., thesis, major research projects) that you believe will enhance your value in the eyes of the recruiter.

Experience

The experience section of your résumé should list your prior employment, highlighting accomplishments that reveal the core skills for which a particular company is searching. The description of each of your accomplishments should include two components: the action you took, and the outcome of your action. To illustrate, "Led cross-functional team from marketing, research and development, operations, and finance to increase market share by 24% and profitability by 18%."

When describing your accomplishments, it is also important to ensure that each accomplishment communicates a particular skill (or set of skills) that enhances your value to the recruiter's company. To illustrate, the above example emphasizes your leadership skills (taking a leadership role), teamwork (the ability to collaborate with other teammates across functions), and management skills (successfully managing complex tasks).

When selecting how to describe your accomplishments, it is also important to ensure that you show breadth of skills, while prioritizing the skills that are crucial to the recruiting company. For example, when applying to consulting companies, underscore your analytical skills while documenting other relevant skills such as leadership, communication, and teamwork.

Additional Information

The additional information section of your résumé (which is sometimes labeled "other skills and accomplishments") should highlight any relevant experiences that demonstrate skills valued by the interviewing company, such as leadership, creativity, teamwork, management skills, and drive. To illustrate, you could include leadership positions, significant involvement in extracurricular activities, and significant accomplishments in sports. It is often useful to include the knowledge of any foreign languages and rate your fluency (e.g., basic, competent, or fluent). You could also include information about your interests and hobbies in cases when you think they reflect a particular skill and/or heighten your fit with the company.

When deciding which information to include, the key is to list only those activities that are likely to enhance your value proposition to the company, rather than list them just to make your résumé longer.

Style and Formatting

Although typically of secondary importance, stylistic and formatting issues, if not adequately implemented, can undermine the impact of your value proposition. Because your résumé is a form of business communication, in addition to summarizing your relevant experiences, it can also be viewed as an indication of your communication skills.

When writing your resume, it is important to use a style that projects an image that is consistent with your value proposition. To achieve that, consider using action verbs that project initiative (see "The Language of Action and Success" following this section).

It is also important to ensure that the résumé clearly communicates your value proposition. It is, therefore, preferable to use simple language and uncomplicated sentence structure. Avoid using professional jargon; your résumé should be impressive, yet easy to understand. Because the résumé is typically restricted to a single page, it is important to optimize the length-to-content ratio of each accomplishment. When describing your activities, be succinct, eliminate all unnecessary words, and focus on content.

In addition to using an appropriate style, it is also important to format your résumé in a way that highlights your accomplishments and at the same time is consistent with commonly accepted formatting guidelines. The overarching rule is that your résumé should be clearly laid out. Do not use creative formatting and fonts that are difficult to read; do not make the font size unreasonably small (e.g., to fit in more information). The focus should be on the content, not on visually distracting details.

The Cover Letter

A well-written cover letter can draw attention to your résumé and may mean the difference between your résumé being considered or disregarded. The cover letter should express your interest in the company and offer a brief overview of your skills and qualifications. Your letter should clearly articulate the reason(s) the company should hire you. It is, therefore, important to underscore your unique value proposition – the core skills that create value to the recruiting company – while differentiating you from the other candidates. When writing the cover letter, think from the recruiters' point of view and try to answer the question they will ask themselves when reading your letter: "Why should we hire this candidate?"

The cover letter should be brief, well-structured, and easy to read. One of the key goals of the cover letter is to motivate the recruiter to read your résumé. A typical mistake many candidates make is trying to include all of their accomplishments in the cover letter. These candidates forget that recruiters are bombarded with hundreds, often thousands, of résumés and cover letters, very few of which are read in great detail. Therefore, the goal of the cover letter is to help you break through the clutter by effectively communicating your unique value proposition. Keep your cover letter short and to the point.

The Résumé as an Introduction to the Personal Experience Interview

One of the most common mistakes in résumé writing is thinking of the résumé as a free-standing document without explicitly considering the impact of the information offered in the résumé on the course of the interview. In fact, interviewers typically rely on the information provided by your résumé to decide which questions to ask you, as well as to determine the overall course of the interview.

To increase the likelihood that you are given the option to demonstrate your value to the recruiter's company, make sure that your résumé prominently features accomplishments that you would like to discuss during the interview. Typically, these events involve accomplishments that best demonstrate the skills you possess that are most valued by recruiters. It is also important to be prepared to elaborate on each point in your résumé.

To help you better position yourself during the interview, provide a clear and understandable description of the nature of the projects with which you were involved, the actions you took, and the results you achieved. Avoid ambiguity in your résumé; do not use terminology and abbreviations that are likely to be unfamiliar to recruiters. Your goal should be to focus the interview on your ability to create value to the recruiter's company rather than spend most of the interview clarifying marginally important points.

Exhibit 1. Résumé Example: Financial Background

RICHARD BESSLER
2001 Sheridan Rd
Evanston, Illinois 60208
(847) 491-3300
rbessler@kellogg.northwestern.edu

EDUCATION

2006-present   **KELLOGG SCHOOL OF MANAGEMENT**   Evanston, IL
NORTHWESTERN UNIVERSITY
Candidate for Master of Business Administration degree, June 2008.
- Cumulative GPA: 4.0/4.0.
- Intended majors in Accounting and Finance.
- Goldman Sachs and Morgan Stanley Fellowship Finalist.
- Elected Investment Banking Club, Finance Club Co-Chair.
- Appointed Graduate Management Association (GMA) International Co-Chair.

1997-2001   **WHARTON SCHOOL, UNIVERSTIY OF PENNSYLVANIA**   New Haven, CT
Bachelor of Arts degree in Business, June 1998. Concentration in Finance.
- Dean's list, graduated cum laude.
- Associate Director, Wharton Peer Advising
- Financed 55% of education through work-study, scholarships, and loans.

EXPERIENCE

2004-2006   **WACHOVIA SECURITIES**   Charlotte, NC
Associate, Public Portfolio Management (Credit Capital Markets)
- Launched healthcare segment of proprietary credit portfolio consisting of over 80 pharmaceutical, biotech, medtech, medical products, and healthcare services companies, representing over $4.5 billion of debt exposure.
- Managed $1.6 billion healthcare portfolio to drive P&L by buying and selling bond, loan, convertible and credit derivative securities.
- Developed research reflecting proprietary investment opinion, industry dynamics, and company's financial and strategic profile for constituents across capital markets' internal platform.

2003-2004   **BANK OF AMERICA**   Chicago, IL
Analyst, Strategic Alliances & Investment (Principal Investing)
- Evaluated and executed strategic private equity investments across bank platform and provided investment, M&A, and JV strategic advisory services.
- Analyzed and directed variety of investment structures, including initial capital outlays, follow-on funding and warrant transactions.
- Supported deal process through due diligence, valuation, execution and post-transaction monitoring of investment.
- Tracked regulatory requirements and prepared investment reviews for 43 holdings representing over $150 million of invested capital.

2001-2003   **GOLDMAN, SACHS & CO.**   New York, NY
Analyst, Investment Banking Division (Mergers & Strategic Advisory Group)
- Advised clients on variety of M&A and financing transactions in consumer products and industrial sectors.
- Developed comprehensive valuation models, including discounted cash flow, merger, leveraged buyout, comparable-company and comparable-transaction analyses.
- Helped both public and private clients to evaluate and develop M&A, takeover defense, corporate structuring, and financing strategies.
- Prepared presentations for senior management groups, boards of directors, and investors, including pitch materials, offering memoranda, fairness opinions and road show presentations.

ADDITIONAL DATA

- Coordinator for St. Thomas's Soup Kitchen, accommodating over 300 people twice a week.
- 2003 NOVA National Mountain Bike Series winner (1st out of 430).

Exhibit 2. Résumé Example: Marketing Background

RYAN HAMILTON
2001 Sheridan Road
Evanston, IL 60208
(847) 491-3300
rhamilton@kellogg.northwestern.edu

EDUCATION

2006-present   **KELLOGG SCHOOL OF MANAGEMENT**   Evanston, IL
NORTHWESTERN UNIVERSITY
Candidate for Master of Business Administration degree, June 2008.
- Cumulative GPA: 3.8/4.0.
- Intended majors in Marketing and Organizational Behavior.
- Elected Marketing Club President, 540 members.

1996 - 2000   **BROWN UNIVERSITY**   Providence, RI
Bachelor of Arts degree in Applied Math-Economics, Bachelor of Arts in History, May 2002.
- Elected Vice President of Education and Treasurer, Brown Investment Group.
- Awarded *Wall Street Journal* Prize for top Economics student.

EXPERIENCE

2000-2006   **THE CLOROX COMPANY**   Oakland, CA
Associate Marketing Manager, Brita, 2004-2006
- Led new brand and advertising strategy development for Brita. Managed $20MM budget.
- Developed insights into new target consumer intended to redefine all marketing communication including: advertising, packaging, consumer promotions, public relations, and in-store merchandising.
- Supervised development of the integrated marketing communications plan for FY06. Managed process and ensured alignment with large cross-functional team, as well as senior management.
- Developed new Brita Hispanic TV commercial ($4MM) and general market Print campaign ($4MM).
- Managed Wal-Mart operations team to influence priorities at Wal-Mart. Led defensive effort to minimize impact of new low-priced competitor in the water filtration category.

Associate Marketing Manager, 409 All Purpose Cleaner, 2002-2004   Oakland, CA
- Managed the repositioning of 409 Lemon to 409 Antibacterial Kitchen, leading to sales gains of +$7MM in customer sales and distribution in an additional 2,500 Wal-Mart stores. Developed dedicated print advertising to support August 2004 launch.
- Analyzed and recommended optimal assortment by retailer, resulting in 15% growth potential.
- Managed 409 refill bottle redesign, projected to deliver $500M/yr in cost savings and enable increased distribution.
- Responsible for "wipes revitalization" plan due to poor market results after launch. Analyzed pricing rollback options to recommended elimination of one scent effective June 2004.

Marketing Associate, Tilex and Liquid Plumr, 2000-2002   Oakland, CA
- Led development of a new Liquid Plumr product with 10% sales growth potential to the franchise. Identified opportunities to conduct unconventional consumer research with a new consumer target.
- Managed cross-functional team to develop Tilex Soap Scum Remover product improvement. Guided team to develop more consumer-relevant technical testing methodology. Team successfully closed performance gap vs. competition, resulting in a consumer-preferred product, (58/42 blind win).
- Created and executed $7MM consumer promotion plan for Tilex and Liquid Plumr. Integrated promotions with overall brand positioning to deliver consumer preference at shelf. Executed $4MM defensive campaign for Tilex that grew dollar share +5 pts in one year.
- Accurately managed Liquid Plumr volume and profit ($75MM in customer sales) during a highly competitive year with three new entrants in the category.

ADDITIONAL DATA
- Fluent in Japanese.
- Finalist in 2001 Mavericks Big Wave Surf Competition (Placed 15 out of 700).
- Special Olympics Track and Field Coach.

Exhibit 3. Résumé Example: Consulting Background

JOANNE FREEMAN
2001 Sheridan Road
Evanston, IL 60208
(847) 491-3300
jfreeman@kellogg.northwestern.edu

EDUCATION

2006-present   **KELLOGG SCHOOL OF MANAGEMENT**   Evanston, IL
NORTHWESTERN UNIVERSITY
Candidate for Master of Business Administration degree, June 2008.
- Cumulative GPA: 4.0/4.0.
- Intended major in Finance.
- Winning team in 9th annual A.T. Kearney Global Prize consulting competition.

1996-2000   **DARTMOUTH COLLEGE**   Hanover, NH
Bachelor of Arts degree in Economics, June 2000.
- Graduated *magna cum laude*
- President, *The Dartmouth Review*.

EXPERIENCE

2005-2006   **ZS ASSOCIATES**   Evanston, IL
Consultant
- Designed a 5-year business strategy across Europe, Asia and the U.S. to facilitate $800MM growth through product integration, strategic account management, manufacturing cost reduction, unprofitable market exits, and increased quality focus.
- Managed a 10-person team over a 2-year period to design and execute the redeployment and market converge initiatives of a 2,000-person sales force for a $5 billion company.

2001-2005   **PRICEWATERHOUSECOOPERS**   Hopewell, VA
Senior Associate 2003-2005 (ranked top 5% of peer group)
- Consulted with top-20 Consumer Finance companies, performing multiple services that included process redesign projects, complex cash flow modeling, and operational risks and controls.
- Managed up to four internal and external staff on project-by-project basis.
- Chosen by Mortgage Bankers Association of America to present on the "Top 5 in '05" at the Mortgage Servicing Conference in Orlando, FL in front of audience of 150 people.
- Selected to lead Small Business team on a Basel II initiative at a large commercial bank.
- Presented on Mortgage Servicing Rights at Executive Enterprise, Inc.'s annual Risk Management Conference in Washington, DC.
- Selected to perform Sarbanes-Oxley review of client's entire mortgage cycle to identify and document all risks, controls, and weaknesses.

Associate 2001-2003   Hopewell, VA
- Designed significant portion of User Acceptance Testing of cash flows for $5 million initiative.
- Led analysis that identified more than $6M in annual benefits for a top-five Mortgage Bank.
- Conducted interviews with all levels of the Servicing Unit at a large Consumer Finance client, which led to the development of cash flow specifications to support a loan-level database.

2000-2001   **MARRIOTT HOTELS**   Reno, NV
Project Manager
- Performed site assessments and conducted reviews and analyses of key performance factors.
- Designed and implemented a cost control and project management program to streamline internal communication and increase information sharing around hotel construction projects.
- Developed market studies that contributed to the creation of a $400 million development plan.

ADDITIONAL DATA
- Fluent in Spanish.
- Cofounder and Chairwoman of Greensoft International Recycling, a non-profit focused on coordinating international technology refurbishing and donation efforts (2003-present).

Exhibit 4. Résumé Example: Engineering Background

BENOÎT GAILLARD
2001 Sheridan Road
Evanston, IL 60208
(847) 491-3300
bgaillard@kellogg.northwestern.edu

EDUCATION

2006-Present   **KELLOGG SCHOOL OF MANAGEMENT**   Evanston, IL
                NORTHWESTERN UNIVERSITY
                Candidate for Master of Business Administration degree, June 2008.
                - Cumulative GPA: 3.9/4.0.
                - Intended majors in Management & Strategy.
                - Winner of 10th annual Carnegie Mellon Operations Management Competition.

1992-1997   **CAMBRIDGE UNIVERSITY**   Cambridge, England
                Master of Engineering degree in Chemical Engineering, June 1997.
                - Awarded University Prize for Research Project: "Light Emitting Diodes" (ranked first of 120).
                - Elected President, Chemical Engineering Society.

                Bachelor of Arts degree in Chemical Engineering, June 1996.
                - Awarded University Prize for Design Project: "Ethanol Recovery " (ranked first of 65).
                - Awarded Junior and Senior Scholarships (1st class Honors exam performance).

EXPERIENCE

2003-2006   **MERCK & COMPANY, INCORPORATED**   Hertfordshire, England
                Senior Engineer, Pharmaceutical Process Technology, 2004-2006
                - Directed a cross-functional team to technically assess outsourcing options for a critical material to capture a five-fold reduction in material costs for a pharmaceutical product.
                - Designed and led execution of an intra-site manufacturing process transfer in Australia that reduced annual discards for a product by more than $1MM.
                - Provided equipment, process, productivity, and troubleshooting support to 9 manufacturing sites worldwide for 7 product families, generating more than $4 billion in annual sales.
                - Spearheaded an operational excellence initiative and led cross-functional team to streamline the use of statistical control for monitoring manufacturing process, reducing discards globally by 9%.

                Lead Technical Engineer, Pharmaceutical Process Technology, 2003-2004
                - Designed the transfer of a new manufacturing process to a Japanese site to support the positioning of a $2 billion/year pharmaceutical product for sale in Japan.
                - Coordinated and executed pilot scale development work for 2 new pharmaceutical products and served as the functional representative on cross-divisional drug development teams.
                - Reduced discards due to quality defects for a $2.4 billion product manufactured at 4 sites by creating a process database and proactively monitoring the data.

1999-2003   **EXXON**   Surrey, England
                Lead Technical Engineer, 2001-2003
                - Managed multiple project teams in developing a state-of-the-art, multimillion dollar semiconductor tester, by facilitating collaboration, as well as providing technical guidance.
                - Led a 10-person team to initiate and execute projects to address a strategic gap, which led to $20 million in additional revenue.
                - Primary contact in R&D to aid customer and marketing teams in new business development.

                Senior Development Engineer, 1999-2001
                - Created innovative approaches to the testing area, leading to the commitment of more than $120 million in revenue from our top target customers.
                - Consulted with customer teams to resolve technical defects and assess customer needs.

ADDITIONAL DATA

                - Fluent French and English, conversational Spanish and German.
                - Authorized to work in U.S.

The Language of Action and Success

Your résumé should project a winning management style; it calls for using active language to effectively communicate your unique value to the company. A number of common action phrases used in résumé writing and during the interview to communicate your achievements are given below:

o Accelerated [performance, development, customer acquisition]

o Accomplished [project, goal, task]

o Achieved a goal

o Administered [contract, project, task]

o Aligned [people to a goal, goal and strategy, strategy and tactics]

o Analyzed [financial impact, organizational fit, data]

o Assessed [risk, impact, competitive threat, market forces]

o Assisted [senior management, clients]

o Awarded [scholarship, grant, prize]

o Bridged a gap

o Capitalized on an opportunity

o Collected [market data, competitive intelligence]

o Completed the project [on schedule, under budget]

o Conceived [idea, strategy, project]

o Conducted [financial, marketing, competitive, sensitivity] analysis

o Coordinated communications to internal and external [constituencies, stakeholders, entities]

o Coordinated team efforts

o Created [a vision, strategy]

o Defined [scope, strategy, implementation plan]

o Designed [strategy, tactics, implementation plan]

o Developed [strategy, marketing plan, vision]

o Devised [program, strategy, project]

o Directed [project, employees, program]

o Established [guidelines, benchmarks, goals]

o Estimated [market potential, competitive response]

o Evaluated new business opportunities

o Evaluated market reaction to [promotions, advertising, price]

o Exceeded a goal

o Executed [strategy, business plan]

o Expanded [operation, project, scope]

o Facilitated [process, acquisition, implementation]

o Formulated [hypotheses, strategy, action plan]

o Fostered collaboration

o Generated [new approach, solutions]

o Identified [strategic gap, opportunities, alternatives, strategies]

o Implemented [program, strategy, goals]

o Improved [communications, customer satisfaction, morale, performance]

o Increased [profits, revenues, sales volume]

o Initiated [project, activity, policy]

o Interacted with [clients, project management, stakeholders]

o Led [product management team, cross-functional teams]

o Managed [project/cross-functional team, the development and implementation of a strategic plan]

o Modified [program, strategy]

o Motivated [team, employees, stakeholders]

o Negotiated [deal, settlement, acquisition]

o Optimized [business model, resource allocation policy, operating structure]

o Outlined [strategy, vision, project]

o Persuaded [clients, management]

o Planned [mergers, strategies, projects]

o Prepared [client reports, presentations]

o Presented [analysis, recommendations, solutions]

o Produced [results, projects, goals]

o Rebuilt [infrastructure, confidence, strategies]

- Reduced [costs, exposure, vulnerability, response time, turnaround time, turnover, uncertainty]

- Resolved a conflict

- Responded to a crisis

- Responsible for [new product development, strategic planning, customer management, project, team, new client development, client account]

- Set [goals, policy]

- Solved a problem

- Streamlined [process, operations, policy]

- Strengthened [reputation, performance]

- Structured [new venture, deal]

- Surpassed [requirements, goals, projections]

- Took [a risk, initiative]

- Won [award, contract, competition]

Chapter Three

The Personal Experience Interview

Overview

The personal experience part of the interview (also referred to as the "behavioral" or "informational" interview) is about getting to know you. There is no fixed format or agenda. This part of the interview usually involves asking you to provide an example of a situation in which you have demonstrated a particular skill (e.g., leadership, analytical, etc.). These questions often begin with "tell me about a time when ..." or "give me an example of...." The goal is to let you demonstrate mastery of the key skills by recounting a relevant story from past experience.

A frequent mistake made by candidates is using general skill descriptors such as "analytic," "creative," and "leadership." It is not uncommon to hear a candidate claiming to be "a natural leader and team player, with analytic and problem-solving skills." As a result, interviewers are likely to hear the same answers repeatedly. This is because most candidates use the same strategy to prepare for interviews: They identify their competencies and attributes, research the industry, company, and job description, and rehearse guidebook answers to typical questions. Therefore, it is important to think from the point of the interviewer, who is faced with a number of candidates, all claiming to have leadership, analytical, and communication skills, to be team players, and to provide the perfect fit for the interviewer's company.

The problem with simply labeling yourself as "analytic," "creative," and "strategic" is twofold. First, these are very general concepts and, as such, they lack specific meaning. Simply stating that you "have analytical skills" does not communicate any relevant information to the interviewer (except that you have figured out that being "analytic" is important). The interviewer cannot even be sure that you actually understand what being "analytic" means. What the interviewer is looking for is a story that reveals a particular skill.

The second concern with using general skill descriptors such as "analytic," "creative," and "strategic" is that recruiting is not just a process of evaluating each candidate but is a *choice* among candidates. Your goal is not only to convince the interviewer that you fit the position requirements but also that you are the *best* among all candidates. Hence, you need to differentiate yourself. Simply saying that you are "analytic," "creative," and a "team player" will not differentiate you, because a great number of other candidates will be rehearsing exactly the same phrases and claiming the same attributes.

A successful interview communicates your value proposition in a meaningful and memorable way that will establish your superiority over the other candidates. This can best be achieved by describing specific instances that vividly demonstrate your particular skills. Tell *your* story, not a textbook example. Your story should be specific and demonstrate your skills in a particular context. Make your story colorful and expressive, which will make it stand out and be more memorable. The interviewer is more likely to relate to a vivid story, and will probably pay closer attention and become more involved in the interview when the story is engaging. The story you tell presents an opportunity to create a positive and lasting impression that will allow the interviewer to later link your story to your name and skills.

Think of the interview as an opportunity to communicate your value proposition while differentiating yourself from other candidates. The interview is a marketing communication task in which you must convince the interviewer that you can satisfy his/her company's needs better than the other candidates. One rarely sees an ad in which a company simply claims product superiority. Instead, a good ad tells you a story that demonstrates the product's benefits in a specific context. You should do the same. The storyboard approach discussed in the following sections shows you how to achieve that.

The Introduction Question

The interview typically starts with an introduction question asking you to offer an overview of who you are, of your career achievements, and/or of your life so far. The prototypical introduction question is "Tell me about yourself." This question is so common that not having a ready answer is inexcusable. Yet, many candidates come to interviews without a prepared answer and instead try to make up an answer on the spot. Even among those who do have a ready answer, many give a textbook cliché introduction, thus failing to take advantage of the opportunity afforded by this question to articulate their value proposition and differentiate themselves from the other candidates. Therefore, it is crucial not only to have a ready introduction, but also to have an introduction that will give you an edge over the other candidates and will bring you closer to receiving an offer.

A useful approach to developing a meaningful introduction is to structure your answer around four key elements: introduction, accomplishments, skills, and value. These four elements, illustrated in Figure 1, can be summarized as follows:

o Start with a brief introduction summarizing your most important and/or most distinct characteristics.

o Briefly summarize your key *accomplishments* to give the interviewer a better picture of what you have achieved so far in your professional career.

o Highlight key *skills* and competencies you have accumulated so far.

o Articulate your *value* to the recruiter's company by linking your skills and accomplishments to your ability to create value for the company better than any of the other candidates.

Figure 1. Structuring Your Introduction Statement

Introduction	Accomplishments	Skills	Value

When preparing for the introduction question, keep in mind that your answer not only gives you the option to articulate your value proposition to the company early on in the interview; it also gives you the option to change the course of the interview by focusing the interviewer's attention on the accomplishments, skills, and value highlighted in your answer. Indeed, it is often the case that issues brought up by candidates in the introduction become the focal points of the interview.

It is also important to keep in mind that in most cases you will not be able to control the pace of the interview; instead you will have to follow the pace set by the interviewer. This implies that you should have several versions of your introduction: a brief version and a few extended ones. However, given that this is an introduction, even the most detailed version of your answer still needs to be short and to the point.

The Storyboard Approach

The storyboard approach introduced here is based on the relatively simple idea of telling vivid and detailed stories to communicate your skills in a specific context. Instead of simply claiming that you have "analytical skills," tell a story that demonstrates how you applied these skills to solve a specific problem. Not only is this more likely to convince the interviewer that you actually have the skill, it will also make you more distinct and your story more memorable.

To make your story engaging, informative, and impactful, you can use the following three-step format, illustrated in Figure 2:

○ Start by describing the decision *context* and the problem that you were trying to solve.

○ Next, describe how you approached the problem and what *actions* you took. Be specific and identify how you were able to solve the problem, what strategy you employed, and how you carried out this strategy. Make sure to underscore how you personally made a difference.

○ Finally, describe the *results*. Quantify the outcome, if possible, and be sure to explain what qualifies that outcome as a success.

Figure 2. The Storyboard Approach to the Personal Experience Interview

The key element in the **context-action-results** (C-A-R) approach is the action step, which often is the focal point of the story. A useful format for presenting a problem-driven action involves the following approach. Start by summarizing what you did to solve the problem and then, time permitting, elaborate on the specific steps describing your action. These include: (1) identifying the problem, (2) generating several possible solution scenarios, (3) gathering additional information, (4) soliciting input from others, (5) selecting the best alternative, (6) designing a plan to implement the proposed solution in a timely manner, and (7) evaluating the results to learn from the experience.

In addition to the context-action-results model, another conceptually similar approach is the **situation-task-action-results**, or S-T-A-R model. Here situation refers to the problem at hand and task refers to your assignment – what you were asked to do or, in cases where you initiated the action, how you interpreted the situation and formulated the task. As can be seen from Figure 3, both the C-A-R and S-T-A-R approaches are essentially identical. Some prefer the C-A-R approach because it is simple and more intuitive. Others prefer to use the S-T-A-R approach because it sounds more relevant to a candidate's situation: Everyone wants to be a "star" in the job market. Ultimately, the choice between the C-A-R and the S-T-A-R approach is arbitrary; use whichever one is more comfortable for you.

Figure 3. C-A-R and S-T-A-R Storyboard Frameworks

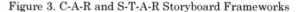
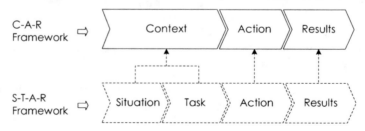

The Skills-in-Context Matrix

The storyboard approach is very useful for illustrating a specific skill (e.g., leadership) in a particular context (e.g., prior job). There are, however, multiple skills that are of interest to interviewers. There are also multiple contexts in which these skills can be shown: prior work experience, prior academic experience, various extracurricular activities, etc. Therefore, it is important to have a system for navigating through different skills in different contexts during the interview. This system is the skills-in-context matrix.

The skills-in-context matrix cross-tabulates the key skills and the different contexts in which these skills can be demonstrated. An illustration of the skills-in-context matrix is shown in Figure 4. The skills factor of the matrix comprises the eight key skills identified in the previous section: leadership, analytical skills, creativity, teamwork, communication skills, management skills, capacity to learn, and drive. The context factor, on the other hand, is represented by the different experiences that provide an environment in which some or all of the above skills might be exhibited.

Figure 4. The Skills-in-Context Matrix

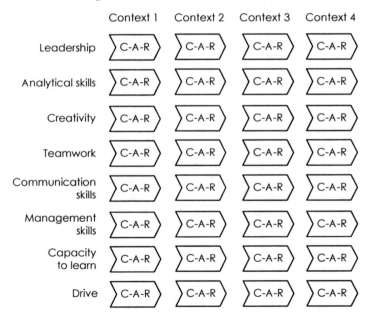

For MBA students, the usual contexts are their college experience, prior job experience(s), MBA program experience (team projects, club involvement, etc.), as well as various extracurricular activities (sports, volunteer work, hobbies, etc.). Some of the contexts, such as prior job experience and academic experience, are typical for all candidates. Others are more specific, and it is up to you to introduce that context during the interview (either in the conversation or by featuring it in the résumé).

A common mistake made by candidates is the lack of a systematic approach to linking specific skills to specific contexts (e.g., analytic skills in college, leadership in prior job, teamwork during the MBA program). As a result, candidates are often unprepared to address interviewers' questions about a specific skill in a particular context (e.g., "tell me about your leadership skills at your most recent job"). To help you avoid making this mistake, the skills-in-context approach calls for a story that demonstrates *each* of the key skills in *each* of the contexts implied by your background. Thus, when asked about a specific skill (e.g., leadership), you will be prepared to tell a story demonstrating this skill across different contexts (skill-based stories). When asked about a specific context (e.g., prior work experience) you have readily available stories that demonstrate your relevant skill set (context-based stories). You will also have a story ready when asked to discuss a specific skill (e.g., leadership) in a particular context (e.g., prior job).

To illustrate, imagine that you have held two jobs prior to enrolling in an MBA program. The natural contexts in which your skills could have been demonstrated are (1) college experience, (2) job #1, (3) job #2, and (4) current MBA experience. To be prepared for the interview, you should be ready to discuss each of the eight key skills in each of the above four contexts. In particular, you should be ready to answer questions about each skill across different contexts as well as questions about different skills demonstrated in a particular context (Figure 5).

Figure 5. Using the Skills-in-Context Matrix

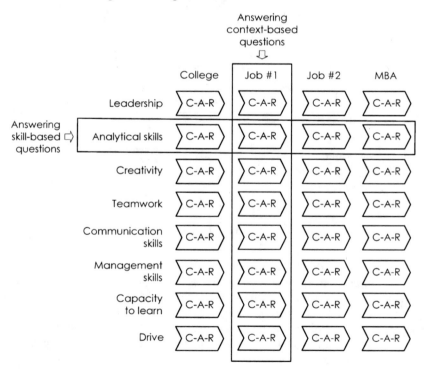

You should also be able to discuss a particular skill in a specific context. To illustrate, if you are asked to talk about your leadership skills at job #2, you should have a ready story that describes the company context, the action taken, and the results (Figure 6).

Figure 6. Using the Skills-in-Context Matrix to Answer a Question about a Specific Skill in a Particular Context

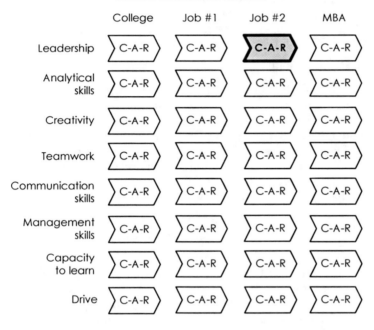

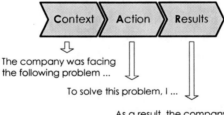

The skills-in-context approach requires a substantial amount of thinking on your part. In many cases it is difficult to come up with examples of different skills in all contexts. Yet, articulating specific instances that demonstrate each relevant skill in different contexts can go a long way to ensure that you have effectively communicated your value proposition to the interviewer.

Typical Opening Questions and Answer Strategies

Most interviews begin with an open-ended general question designed to break the ice and set the tone for the interview. The introduction question also gives candidates an opportunity to state their value proposition early in the interview. Answer strategies to some of the most common introduction questions are given below.

○ Tell us about yourself.

This is the prototypical question to start the interview. Prepare a narrative that highlights who you are and, most important, your unique value proposition to the interviewing company. You cannot avoid this question and should have a ready answer for it. In fact, even if not asked, you should still work the answer into the interview (e.g., "it might be helpful if I start by providing my background"). Prepare a one-, three-, and five-minute version of your story so that you have the option to choose the narrative that best fits the interview timeframe.

○ Walk me through your résumé and explain the decisions you have made to date (Variation of this question: Describe your career progression to date).

This is a straightforward question and you should be able to answer it in about two minutes, but be prepared to go into much greater depth, if asked. As you walk the interviewer through your résumé, make sure to use your accomplishments to underscore your value proposition to the company (i.e., why the company should hire you).

○ Why would you like to work for us?

You should have an answer for this question. If you can't answer it, you should take this company off your list.

○ Why should we hire you?

Offer a brief summary of your value proposition. Describe the key assets and competencies that you bring to the firm. You can organize them around the three key factors: skills, knowledge, and fit with the company.

○ Why did you decide to get an MBA, and why did you choose to do it at this school?

Your answer should focus on your ambitions to grow professionally. Explain why the school you have chosen to attend is the best fit for you given your current skills and long-term goals.

Questions Testing Your Core Skills

The eight basic core skills for which companies are looking are: leadership, analytical skills, creativity, teamwork, communication, management, capacity to learn, and drive. Examples of common interview questions for each of these skills are given below.

▸ Leadership

o Give an example of your ability to build motivation in your co-workers, classmates, or a volunteer committee.

o What leadership roles have you played prior to applying for a position with our company?

o Have you ever had an idea or a goal to achieve something that required action by other people? How did you implement this idea?

o Describe a situation in which you led a group to complete a complex assignment and motivated others to get the work done on time.

o How would you build a team from independent individuals?

o How do you motivate people?

o How do you help ensure that your team meets project deadlines?

o Describe a situation demonstrating your ability to foster teamwork early on and prove that you have the potential to become a team leader.

o How did you foster effective and open communication and achieve your and your teammates' goals?

o How did you build a shared vision and shared goals?

o How did you resolve differences of opinion and group tensions?

o How did you instill in others an atmosphere of support, responsiveness, and respect?

o Describe a situation in which you were in charge of a group of people and moved something forward. How did you mobilize the team to work toward achieving the result you chose?

▸ Analytical Skills

o Tell me about your analytical skills.

o You seem to have strong analytical skills. Why do you believe you can handle the requirements of the job you are applying for?

o Tell me about a complex problem you had to solve, and walk me through your thinking as you solved it.

- Describe a situation in which you took a complex problem and designed an actionable strategy to solve this problem.
- Describe a situation in which you had to make an important decision without having all the necessary information at hand.
- How would you describe your approach to solving problems?
- Describe a situation in which you had to apply your skills to learn a new technology or a process.

▸ Creativity

- In your work experience, what have you done that you consider truly creative?
- How would you define creativity?
- Would your friends/colleagues describe you as a creative person?
- Tell me about a creative solution that you developed for a difficult problem.
- Describe a situation in which you developed a unique and resourceful solution to a difficult problem.
- Describe a situation that demonstrates your ability to see multiple options or look at things from a different point of view.
- Which of your creative accomplishments has given you the most satisfaction?

▸ Teamwork

- How would your team members describe you?
- Describe a recent unpopular decision you made and the results of this decision.
- Do you prefer to work by yourself or with others?
- What makes for a good team member?
- What types of people do you have trouble getting along with?
- What was the most challenging group you successfully worked with?
- How do you determine the role you play on the team?
- Tell me three positive and three negative things your team members would say about your interactions with them.
- What is the most difficult thing for you in working with your team members?

o What makes you most effective with people? What kinds of people do you find most challenging? What conflicts or difficulties do you experience?

o Describe a specific experience working in a group or team situation where there was interpersonal conflict. Describe how you approached the conflict, what worked well, and what did not. How did you manage the outcome?

▸ Communication Skills

o Tell me about a situation in which you had to speak up or be assertive in order to get an important point across.

o How would you define good communication skills?

o How would you rate your communication skills? What have you done to improve them?

o Describe a time when you had to change your communication style to deliver a message or get your point across.

o Describe the most important document, report, or presentation that you had to complete.

o Give me some examples of how you have adapted your own style to deal with different people and situations.

o Would you rather write a report or give a verbal report? Why?

o How would you rate your writing abilities? Your listening skills?

o Describe a time when you tried to persuade another person to do something that he/she was not eager to do.

o Describe a situation in which you experienced ineffective communication. What would you do differently in this situation?

o Sell me this pen (bottle of water, computer, etc.).

▸ Management Skills

o Give an example of what you've done when your time schedule or project plan was upset by unforeseen circumstances.

o Tell me about a recent crisis you handled.

o Do you work well under pressure? Can you make fast decisions?

o Do you manage your time well?

o How do you handle different priorities in your life (e.g., family, work, school, sports)?

o Describe a situation in which you recognized a problem or an opportunity. How did you respond? Did you choose to address this situation on your own? What obstacles did you face and how did you overcome them?

- How do you make important decisions?
- How do you manage risk?
- What do you do when you are having trouble with a project?
- What was your most difficult decision in the last six months? What made it difficult?
- Your boss (client) tells you to do something you believe is wrong. What do you do?
- Describe a situation in which you had to make an important decision without having all the necessary information at hand.
- Describe a situation demonstrating your ability to transition quickly and effectively between different tasks.
- How did you shift priorities and modify actions to meet changing job demands on short notice?
- How did you prepare for this interview?

▶ Capacity to Learn

- Describe a difficult situation that you feel you should have handled differently. What did you learn from that experience?
- You have had little experience with marketing (finance, technology, etc.). How do you intend to learn what is required from the position you are applying for?
- How do you handle change?
- Are your grades a good measure of your ability to learn?
- If hired, you will be working with experienced individuals who have been with the company for many years. What makes you think that your performance will be on a par with theirs?
- In what areas do you need to develop professionally? How do you plan to achieve that?

▶ Drive

- Give me examples of projects or tasks you started on your own.
- Give me an example of how you demonstrated initiative.
- What are your most important long-term goals? What aspirations do you have for yourself over the next five or so years — professionally and personally?

o Where do you see yourself in two (five, ten) years?

o What does "success" ("failure") mean to you?

o Describe a situation in which you aspired to reach a goal. What obstacles confronted you along the way? What did you do to overcome them?

o Tell me about a time you hit a wall trying to push forward a great idea.

o Describe a situation that demanded sustained, unusually hard work, where others might have thought you couldn't succeed. Was the experience stressful? If so, how did you handle the stress?

Questions Testing Your Functional Knowledge

There are two basic types of functional knowledge questions: questions probing your theoretical knowledge (e.g., frameworks, models, and concepts) and questions calling for specific examples to illustrate a particular concept. Examples of common interview questions from each of these two types are given below.

▸ Conceptual Questions

o You're launching a new product line for our company. Walk me through your decision on how to structure pricing (advertising, distribution, service).

o A brand is very powerful in one product category of the supermarket. How do you determine whether to leverage the brand in another category? (i.e., Should Coke enter the ice cream market?)

o How do you determine whether or not to extend your product line?

o If your brand manager asks you to write a marketing plan for the next year, what would the table of contents look like?

o Which is more profitable, a 10% increase in price or a 10% increase in share?

o What would you do to double a company's market share?

o What are the 10 most important questions that you would ask to learn about a brand on your first day of work as a brand manager?

o You are the brand manager of Company X and you need a new product to drive the top line. Where do you go?

o How would you evaluate the success of an advertising campaign?

o Is Super Bowl advertising a good value?

▸ Example Questions

o Name a product you think is marketed (advertised) well.

o Identify one good and one bad commercial.

o Identify a website that markets consumer goods well.

o Identify a brand that you feel is (is not) marketed well. Why is it (isn't it) marketed well?

o Tell me about a new product introduction you liked. What would you have done differently to market the product?

o Tell me about a poor product that was marketed well. What would you have done differently to the product?

o Identify a company that has made a huge strategic error. Why was it an error?

Questions Testing Your Fit with the Company

There are three basic dimensions of your fit with the company: personality fit, commitment to the company, and commitment to the functional area. Examples of common interview questions from each of these types are given below.

▸ **Personality Fit**

o What experiences/skills do you feel are particularly transferable to our organization?

o What type of work do you like to do best?

o What accomplishments have given you the greatest satisfaction?

o Describe one of your most defining experiences.

o What was the most important thing your parents (prior job experiences) taught you?

o Other than money, what makes you happy at work?

o If you could have dinner with anyone, dead or alive, who would it be and why?

o How do you spend your spare time? What is your favorite hobby? Name a book you've recently read. What movies have you recently seen?

o Have you heard anything about our company that you do not like?

o How would you fit with our corporate culture?

o What do you consider more important: a high salary or career advancement?

o What characteristics should we be looking for in the "ideal" candidate for our company?

▸ **Commitment to the Company**

o Why would you choose our firm over our competitors?

o Why do you want to work for our company?

o How long do you plan to stay with our company?

o Is there anything that will prevent you from taking a position with our company?

o With what other firms are you interviewing?

o Which other industries are you considering?

o Which of our company's products would you like to market? Why?

- Who is our main competitor?

- How would you improve the performance of our company?

- Where do you think our industry is going? What are the key trends and how would they impact our company?

▶ Interest in the Functional Area

- Why would you like to pursue a career in consulting (marketing)?

- Why are you interested in marketing/brand management?

- What brands do you feel passionately about and why?

- Which three items would you take with you to "Brand Manager Island"?

Discussing Strengths, Weaknesses, and Mistakes

Some of the most common interview questions involve asking candidates to identify their strengths, weaknesses, successes, and mistakes. Examples of such questions and possible answer strategies are given below.

o Identify your key *strengths*.

This is an easy question for most candidates. The key issue here is to underscore the strengths that fit the company needs.

There are many variations of the same question: What makes you special? How would you describe yourself? How would your friends (teammates, boss) describe you? If you had a blank billboard on which to create an ad for yourself, how would you fill the billboard? If you created an advertisement for yourself for this position, what would it be like? Which brand best fits your personality and why? Describe your strengths and how you would position yourself in the marketplace.

o Identify your key *weaknesses*.

This is a difficult, as well as a very tricky, question. Everyone has weaknesses, but you do not want them to hinder your chance of getting an offer. There is no common approach to this question; however, it is important to have a ready answer.

As a general rule, you might consider not emphasizing weaknesses that reflect a major deficiency in the skills required for the position you are applying for, weaknesses that could potentially result in significant damage to your employer, and weaknesses for which you cannot clearly articulate how you intend to successfully overcome their potential limitations.

One possible answer strategy when talking about your weaknesses is to state that you have no shortcomings that will prevent you from doing an excellent job and being an asset to your interviewer's company. An alternative strategy is to put a positive spin on the question: Instead of talking about weaknesses, identify areas in which you are likely to perform your best (which implicitly identifies some areas in which you might not be that strong). In most cases, it is a good idea to avoid clichés of the type: "I work too much."

Overall, it is important to keep in mind that selectively identifying your weaknesses has important ethical implications. Thus, if you think that you have major deficiencies, instead of hiding them from your employer, you should consider working on them to improve your performance prior to the interview.

o What are your three (two, one) most important *accomplishments*? Why?

This is a straightforward question: Pick accomplishments that most clearly communicate your value to the company.

○ What is your greatest *failure*?

This is another difficult question requiring a well-thought-out answer. The goal is to identify a failure that does not hinder your chance of getting an offer. In general, you might want to avoid failures that resulted in a significant damage (e.g., financial loss, negative publicity, loss of a client) to your employer, failures that reflect a major deficiency in the skills required for the position you are applying for, failures that are too recent and from which you have not had a chance to learn, as well as failures for which you cannot clearly articulate the lessons learned and, instead, provide an example of a scenario in which you successfully resolved a similar problem.

One strategy to address this question is to embed your failure in a context that turns this failure into a valuable experience. This approach, summarized in Figure 7, calls for a brief description of the failure, which is then followed by a summary of the lessons learned from that experience and a success story demonstrating how you applied the lessons learned from the failure to your advantage. Conclude your story by identifying how the lessons learned from your failure enhances your value to the company.

Figure 7: Framing a Failure as a Learning Experience

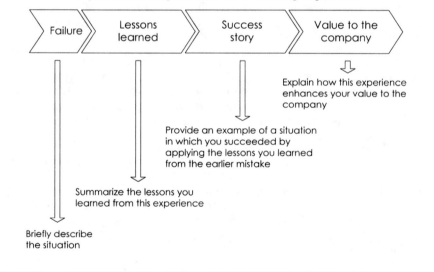

Chapter Four

The Case Interview

Being a successful manager requires the ability to deal creatively with complex problems and to reach logical conclusions based on the available facts in a short timeframe. Because no particular background or set of qualifications prepares candidates for that, many companies have come to rely on the case analysis approach as an integral part of the interview process.

Case interviews test your ability to solve problems on the spot. Case analysis not only allows interviewers to examine your ability to think logically and articulate an answer, it also allows them to observe your thought processes, tolerance for ambiguity and data overload, poise, self-confidence, and communication skills under pressure. For that reason, case analysis is an important part of the interview. As an additional benefit, the interactive nature of the case interview adds a dynamic dimension to understanding your personality and allows better evaluation of your fit with the interviewer's company.

Case analysis can involve two types of problems: business cases and brainteasers. Business cases deal with business problems such as profitability, market share, mergers and acquisitions, new product launch decisions, etc. Brainteasers, in contrast, deal with logical problems across different, typically non-business, contexts. These two types of cases are discussed in more detail in the following sections.

Business Cases

Case analysis examines your approach to a complex situation and tests skills and competencies to identify and solve complex problems. Case analysis places particular emphasis on factors that are more difficult to test in the context of the traditional interview. These factors include logical reasoning and quantitative analysis (analytical skills), creative problem solving (creativity), the ability to clearly express your point of view (communication skills), and professional poise and ability to perform under pressure (management skills).

In a case interview, you are introduced to a particular business scenario and asked to analyze the situation and offer a solution. The interview proceeds as an open dialogue between you and the interviewer in which your goal is to identify the source of the problem and recommend a solution.

The key issue to keep in mind is that case analysis is not about the solution per se; it is about how you arrive at that solution. Rather than looking for one specific answer, interviewers are trying to understand how you think. In this context, the interviewer is more interested in your assumptions, your selection of a framework, and the quality of your reasoning than in whether you arrive at the "right answer" (which, as a matter of fact, often does not exist).

A good strategy for approaching case analysis is to think of the interview as a problem-solving task in which you work through hypothetical business problems. Try to forget that this is an interview and think of it as a consulting assignment in which the interviewer is the client. Your goal should be to solve your client's problem rather than guess at the "right" answer. Remember that the interviewer wants to hire a person who will be solving business problems on a day-to-day basis and feels comfortable with the process.

Business Case Format

Business cases can be presented in one of two formats: oral and written. These two formats are discussed in more detail below.

Oral cases are presented in an interactive manner: They offer very little information up front and leave it up to you to uncover the case specifics. Oral cases are very popular among recruiters, especially during the early rounds of interviews, because they provide excellent insights into candidates' ability to identify the relevant information, decision processes, and interpersonal skills. Business problems are often phrased as "CEO questions" or "client questions." For example: "You are the CEO of a telecommunications company and your profits are falling despite the overall category growth. What do you do?" or "You have been hired to advise a major consumer goods company that is considering launching a new line of lunch cereals. How would you advise your client?"

In addition to the typical business problems, interviews can involve behavioral cases that deal with relationship-building and team-management issues. A common behavioral case involves a client project in which something has gone wrong, and the goal is to resolve the problem, control the damage, and deal with the team and/or the client. You might be asked to explain what you will do to resolve the situation or, alternatively, you might be asked to role play the interaction.

Written cases are usually several pages long and are accompanied by data exhibits that contain supplemental information. Candidates are usually given time to read the case and prepare for a discussion. Written cases offer insights into your ability for logical reasoning and quantitative skills, as well as the ability to interpret complex data patterns, usually presented in the form of a chart and/or a table. The goal is to assess candidates' ability to interpret data presented in different formats and their ability to derive conclusions from these data. This type of case is often used by recruiters during advanced rounds of the interview, although some consulting companies tend to use written cases during the early rounds as well.

Written cases can also be tested in both an individual and group context. In a group case analysis, each of the candidates is given a written case and a set of specific questions to be answered. After reading the case, candidates take part in a group discussion in which they present their solution and comment on the solutions presented by other team members. Recruiters are looking for candidates who can present their own findings, integrate the input from other team members, and comment on the solutions presented by other team members. In this context, group interviews are a litmus test for your leadership abilities, interpersonal skills, and collaborative spirit.

Common Case Problems

Based on the nature of the underlying task, most cases can be divided into three basic types: (1) action-planning cases, (2) performance-gap cases, and (3) external-change cases. These three case types are discussed in more detail below.

Action-planning cases typically involve the development of a course of action to achieve a certain goal. To illustrate, planning cases involve questions such as developing an overall marketing plan for launching a new product offering and developing a pricing, communication, and/or distribution strategy.

Performance-gap cases depict a company faced with a discrepancy between the desired and the actual state of affairs, between the goal and the reality. To illustrate, a decline in an offering's market share can be viewed as a performance gap between the company's desire to strengthen its market position (goal) and the decrease in market share (reality). Other examples of performance gaps include discrepancies between desired and actual net income, profit margins, and revenues.

External-change cases depict a company faced with a change in the environment in which it operates. To illustrate, external change cases involve questions such as evaluating the impact of a new competitive entry, a competitive action (e.g., new product introduction, price change, aggressive promotions, superiority claims), changes in customer demand, changes in technology, legal regulations, and government policies.

Examples of action-planning, performance-gap, and external-change cases can be found at the end of this chapter.

How to Approach the Case

The case interview typically starts with a brief description of a business scenario such as a client facing declining market share, eroding profit margins, or a new product introduction. Recruiters are not looking for candidates who happen to know the right answer and can "crack the case," but rather for people who have a system that will allow them to solve *any* case. Indeed, even though each problem requires its own unique analysis, most companies believe that the process of analyzing various business problems has a common structure that carries across different scenarios. Therefore, when discussing the case, it is important to apply a logical, well-structured approach that enables you to reach a meaningful conclusion.

A common approach to case analysis includes four steps: clarify, structure, analyze, and conclude. These four steps to case analysis are logically connected (Figure 1). First, determine the situation, identify the problem, and verify the facts; next, develop and present a framework for analyzing the problem; then, apply the framework to analyze specific problems and derive effective solutions; and finally, make a recommendation. These steps are outlined in more detail below.

Figure 1. Structuring the Case Analysis

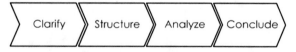

o *Clarify.* The first step is to make sure that you understand the business scenario and the question you are being asked. In fact, one of the most common mistakes during a case interview is misunderstanding the question or answering the wrong question. Sometimes the interviewer will deliberately interject ambiguity into the problem as a part of the interview. Ask clarification questions if you are unclear about certain aspects of the case. A simple strategy to start case analysis is to paraphrase the question to ensure that you understand the problem.

o *Structure.* Structuring involves choosing an approach (framework) to solve the problem. It is a good idea to describe your overall approach and explain the logic used to address the problem. Try to find the appropriate framework to break the problem into separate issues, but do not force-fit a framework to the problem. Remember that your goal is not to showcase your knowledge of a particular framework but to demonstrate your ability to solve business problems. Frameworks are tools to help you organize your thinking; they are not the solution to the problem. It is a good idea to explain the reasons for selecting the framework you use and how you would go about applying the framework to the problem at hand. Remember that recruiters are not particularly interested in your solution to the problem at hand; instead, they are interested in your ability to apply a systematic approach to solving diverse business problems.

○ *Analyze.* There are three basic components to a solid analysis: facts, assumptions, and logic.

- *Facts* are the cornerstones of your analysis and are used to derive your assumptions, logical conclusions, and proposed actions. Some of the facts might not be readily available, and you will have to ask the interviewer to fill in the gaps. As a general rule, the shorter the case, the greater the likelihood that you will have to request additional information as you analyze the problem.

- *Assumptions* are necessary to fill in the missing facts. Making assumptions is a common practice in business analysis; the key is to ensure that your assumptions are realistic and clearly articulated. Use sensitivity analysis (e.g., compare an aggressive vs. a conservative scenario) when unsure about the validity of a particular assumption (e.g., market share growth, rate of new product adoption).

- *Logic* links the available information (facts and assumptions) to uncover new relationships (e.g., cause-and-effect), derive conclusions (e.g., if ... then...), and/or apply general business principles to the case at hand (e.g., an increase in price is likely to lead to a decrease in quantity sold). Break the problem into separate issues, address the issues one at a time, and state findings for each analysis. Remember that the interview is not about the outcome (i.e., getting the "right" answer) but about the process of getting the problem solved. Walk the interviewer through your thinking, and use visual aids (flowchart, matrix, bullet points) when possible.

○ *Conclude.* Conclude the case discussion by summarizing your logic and offering a recommendation that reflects your decision on how the company should address the situation described in the case. The proposed solution should be clear and based on your evaluation of facts, assumptions, and logic, rather than on unsubstantiated opinions. Link your recommendation back to the problem and identify how your solution will solve the problem.

Brainteaser Cases

Brainteaser questions seek to directly test your creative problem-solving and logical reasoning skills. While not all interviewers use brainteasers, they are very common among management consulting and software companies. Unlike traditional business cases, brainteasers usually are abstract questions describing a specific, typically non-business problem. Although some questions might require certain factual knowledge, most brainteasers are self-contained logical tasks. There are three main types of brainteasers: (1) estimation cases (e.g., How many piano tuners are there in the world?), (2) logical cases (e.g., Why do Coke cans have an indent on the bottom?), and

(3) creative cases (e.g., How would you move Mount Fuji?). These three types of brainteasers are described in more detail in the following sections.

Estimation Cases

The popularity of estimation cases in management consulting interviews stems from the fact that these questions are not only easy to create, discuss, and evaluate, but also that they are representative of the type of problems managers and consultants face in their day-to-day work. Estimation questions typically require both logical deduction and quantitative skills. Their goal is not to test factual knowledge but, instead, to observe your approach to problem solving. In this context, the answer, per se, is often irrelevant; what counts is the process of arriving at the answer.

Estimation cases can vary from market sizing problems in which you have to determine the size of a particular market (e.g., What is the size of the market for the Segway human transporter?) to estimating physical factors such as weight and volume (e.g., How much does the moon weigh?).

Estimation tasks can sometimes be part of a more comprehensive case analysis. To illustrate, the answer to the question of whether a company should launch a new product largely depends on the size of the potential market.

While each estimation question is likely to have its unique set of solutions, two general approaches to estimation questions can be identified: analysis and analogy.

o *Estimation by analysis* involves breaking down the object into smaller parts and estimating each part individually. For example, in the case of estimating the weight of an airplane, one might break down the problem into a series of more specific tasks such as estimating the weight of the different parts of the airplane: the body, engines, fuel, luggage, passengers, etc.

o *Estimation by analogy* involves comparing the estimated object to a similar object with known parameters. To illustrate, when asked to estimate the number of car batteries annually sold in the United States, one can use total car sales to arrive at the answer.

Estimation cases might require certain factual knowledge to derive the final answer. Knowing the facts helps, but it is not crucial. Remember, the goal of the interview is not to test whether you can get the "right" answer but to test your ability for logical reasoning. Therefore, if you do not have the necessary data readily available, describe the *process* you would use to solve the problem. In most cases, describing the algorithm is more important than running the actual calculations.

Logic Cases

Logic cases typically describe an abstract problem based on logical reasoning. The goal is to uncover the logical principle underlying the problem. Unlike estimation and creative questions, most logical problems have a unique solution. To illustrate, consider the classic problem: Why do Coke cans have an indent on the bottom? More examples of logic questions can be found at the end of this chapter.

Creative Cases

Creative cases are another form of brainteasers and are very popular among companies in which creativity is paramount (e.g., software, design, product development, and advertising). By definition, creative cases can be about virtually anything. To illustrate, consider the following questions: How would you describe green to a blind person? How would you design a mobile phone for dogs? How would you design a restroom for a CEO? How would you develop a technology to grow straight bananas? How would you describe a pineapple to a person who has never seen one? How would you describe the business school of the future? These questions test your creativity and ability to think "outside of the box" to find an original solution to a non-trivial problem. An additional benefit of creative questions is that they lend themselves to interesting conversation that can provide further insights into your personality.

Preparing for a Brainteaser Interview

Because brainteaser questions lack a pre-set format, topic, and structure, one cannot really "prepare" for a brainteaser interview (which is one of the reasons that interviewers like these questions!). Practicing, however, can help you better articulate your decision process, improve your logical thinking, and help you develop your own strategy for approaching brainteaser questions.

Winning Case Interview Strategies

Mastering the case analysis requires the ability to deal creatively with complex problems and to reach logical conclusions, based on the available information, in a short period of time. The interactive nature of case analysis adds a dynamic dimension to the interview by letting the recruiter observe your poise, self-confidence, and communication skills under pressure. A set of winning strategies on how to manage the problem-solving and the interactive aspects of the case interview are outlined below.

▸ Solving the Case

o Make sure you are answering the question you have been asked; ask questions if you are unsure about the details. Misunderstanding the question or answering the wrong question is one of the most common mistakes in a case interview.

o Remember that rarely are you given all the case information up front. You are expected to ask intelligent questions that will reveal the relevant information that is not readily available.

o Be systematic. Finish one key question and summarize the findings before you go on to the next. Step back periodically to summarize what you have learned so far and how it relates to the problem you are trying to solve. Do not proceed in a haphazard fashion, jumping from one issue to another.

o Use frameworks creatively. Do not force-fit a familiar framework to a problem (one of the most common case analysis mistakes). The key is to use common sense.

o Always focus on the big picture: Solve the problem without getting stuck in details. Prioritize issues. Start with factors that are likely to have the greatest impact. There is no need to mention the framework you will be using by name; instead, explain the structure of your analysis so that the interviewer understands your thought process.

o When given a complex problem, think broadly and be sure to cover all relevant issues rather than spending all your time on one particular issue (unless the interviewer asks you to do so).

o Stay away from phrases like "as we learned in our strategy class..." and "the textbook says that..." to justify your decisions. You should be able to explain and justify the logic for your arguments on your own.

o Do not be afraid to think "outside the box." There is no box. Creativity and brainstorming may be just what the interviewer is seeking. Use business judgment, logic, and common sense.

o Identify the assumptions you are making to solve the problem. Explain the rationale for making these assumptions and their consistency with the facts of the case. Always clarify whether you are making assumptions of your own or restating the case facts.

o When possible, use visual aids to support your analysis. Draw flowcharts to represent business processes; use bullet points to highlight different aspects of the case; use matrixes to represent more complex relationships between factors with multiple levels.

o When possible, use calculations to support your analysis. This is an opportunity to demonstrate your quantitative skills.

▶ **Interacting with the Interviewer**

o Listen carefully and take notes. Remember that you are not expected to have a ready solution to the case problem; when necessary, take a moment to collect your thoughts.

o Think out loud. The interviewer wants to know your thought process, not just the solution. If you have rejected some alternatives, explain why so that the interviewer has a better understanding of your thought process.

o Structure your answer by explaining your strategy (framework) up front so that the interviewer knows what you are trying to do.

o Be confident, even if you do not know the answer to a specific question. It is important for the interviewer to understand that you know how to react if a client asks you something you do not know.

o Remember that "cracking the case" does not mean finding the "right" answer (which rarely exists). It is all about how you analyze the problem.

o Interact with the interviewer. The case should be a dialogue, not a monologue.

o Be flexible in defending your point. The interviewer might disagree with you in order to test your reaction to being challenged. Keep an open mind and watch for cues from the interviewer.

o Think of the interviewer as your client. The interview is a test of your ability to interact with the client in a way that allows you to better understand the problem and make a sound recommendation.

o Have fun. Interviewers are looking for people who enjoy solving problems and are fun to work with. Think of case analysis as an opportunity to discuss novel ideas and address challenging problems with smart people.

o The best way to ensure that all of the above issues come to you naturally during the interview is to practice. Practice solving different cases to become more comfortable with the process.

Business Case Examples

Most business cases can be classified into on of three types: action-planning cases, performance-gap cases, and external-change cases. Examples of common interview questions for each of these types of cases are given below.

▶ Action-Planning Cases

○ You are charged with marketing a candy bar that has been very successful in France. What things should you consider in bringing the product to market in the United States?

○ A start-up software company is preparing to launch its first product. How should it balance customer service and sales force resources?

○ Your client has developed a new statistical software package. How would you price it?

○ A music company has asked your advice on how to price a soon-to-be released record of a new artist. How would you respond?

○ Your client, Cingular Wireless, is trying to determine which customer segments it should target in order to increase revenues. What would you advise?

○ Your client is considering launching a new product. What should you consider in bringing the product to market?

○ How would you go about developing a pricing strategy for a large ski resort?

○ Your client is ready to launch a new product that is both a pen and a USB flash drive. Should she distribute this product to office supply stores or to computer stores?

○ The CEO of a start-up biotech company has asked your advice in developing a business plan. How would you approach this assignment?

○ We have many product upgrades, but it is hard to encourage customers to buy the new product because the original is still useful. How do you encourage customers to buy new upgrades of the product?

○ A department store in Chicago is buying an equally prestigious department store in another city and changing that store's name to match its own. How would you handle changing the name of the store?

○ You are the CEO of a Fortune 500 company that is spending $500M on advertising each year. How do you know if this is a worthwhile investment? What would you do next year: Would you increase the advertising budget, decrease it, or leave it unchanged?

▸ **Performance-Gap Cases**

○ A computer manufacturer is experiencing declining sales. Its product is superior in lifetime and quality to its competitors' products. What would you do?

○ A shoe manufacturer is gaining market share but has experienced declining profits. What would you do?

○ You are a product manager for product X. For the past few years, the share of your company has been decreasing even though the overall category was flat. What would you do?

○ You are the brand manager of a product whose sales have been flat for the last five years. However, the brand's market share has been growing by 5% per year. What's happening with this particular brand and what would you do about it?

○ A company's market share is decreasing and the two options on the table are to lower the price or to advertise. What would you do?

○ You are the CEO of a large software company. You notice that one of your soft-ware products is losing money. What would you do?

○ Your client, the leading soft drink manufacturer in Brazil, is losing share to one of its competitors. How would you advise your client?

○ Your client is losing money because of the large number of incoming customer calls. What would you advise?

○ You are the director of the San Francisco Opera. Ticket sales are down. What would you do?

○ Your client, a major retail broker, is faced with a declining customer base. How would you address this problem?

○ Your client, a major satellite radio company, has a problem attracting new customers. What would you advise?

○ Your client would like to increase its profit margins by 6%. What would be your advice?

○ Your client, McDonald's, is concerned that its growth has been slower than expected. How would you advise the company?

○ Your client, Eastman Kodak Company, is facing declining sales of its traditional film products due to the growth of digital photography. What would you advise?

○ Your market share has been declining for the past year. What would you do?

○ Your client, a large computer game manufacturer, has a difficult time convincing software programmers to develop games for its platform. How would you address this problem?

▸ **External-Change Cases**

○ Your competitor just lowered its price. What do you do?

○ Your competitor just launched an aggressive advertising campaign. What do you do?

○ What would you do if R&D told you that they had come up with a pasta sauce that lowers cholesterol?

○ How should Fatburger (fast food chain) react to consumers' obsession with fat-free food?

○ How should Segway react to state laws restricting the use of Segways on side-walks?

○ Your client, a large sports club, is successfully operating in an upscale urban neighborhood. A developer announces plans to build a residential complex nearby that will also include a sports club that will directly compete with your client's club. How would you advise your client?

○ Your brand has experienced substantial share erosion for the past several years because of a competitor that claims to be "better." Under what circumstances should you reformulate your product?

○ Your client is a high-end sports car manufacturer that is concerned about vulnerability to market cycles. What is your advice?

○ What is the impact of rising gasoline prices on McDonald's sales?

○ Your client makes hydraulic pumps and is concerned about vulnerability to market cycles. What should it do?

○ Our client is a regional retail bank that has recently faced increased competition from new Internet-based financial services firms. Deposits are decreasing, and the client is looking to grow its bottom line. As a consultant, how would you advise the client?

○ For the last 20 years you have been the only major parcel delivery service in Australia. Recently a new firm entered the market, and while it has only stolen 15% of market share, your profits are down by almost 25%. How would you address the situation?

○ You are the CEO of an old tire manufacturing plant. How do you regard the threat of a competitor that has built a new facility in the same area?

○ Discover has faced strong competition from new credit cards entering the market and is considering dropping its $50 annual fee. Is this a good idea?

○ Your client is a large national telephone company that is concerned about losing share to new broadband phone companies. Is this a valid concern? What advice would you have for the client?

Estimation Cases: Problems and Solutions

Estimation cases are a form of brainteaser commonly given in interviews to test logical thinking and analytical skills.

o How many golf balls does it take to fill up an Olympic swimming pool?

The popular solution is to compare the volume of the swimming pool and the golf ball. Given that the pool is 50 meters x 25 meters x 3 meters, its volume is 3,750 cubic meters, or 228,837,667 cubic inches. The golf ball's volume is 2.48 cubic inches (the radius of the golf ball is 0.84 inches and the formula for measuring the volume of a sphere is: [4 x (Pi) x radius cubed]. Given that the densest packing of spheres possible is 74%, it can be calculated that it takes 68.28 million golf balls to fill the pool. Note, however, that this solution requires very specific knowledge (e.g., the formula for measuring the volume of a sphere and the maximum density packing coefficient) and, hence, is not readily applicable to most business interviews.

An alternative solution does not require knowing complex formulas. The size of an Olympic pool is 50 meters x 25 meters x 3 meters. The diameter of a golf ball is 1.68 inches or .0427 meters (1 inch = 2.54 centimeters). Therefore, it will take 685,000 golf balls to cover the bottom of the pool (1,171 x 585). The depth of the pool is 3 meters or 70 golf balls. Therefore, when golf balls are stacked up by putting each layer precisely on top of one another, the swimming pool will accommodate approximately 47.95 million balls (685,000 x 70). Note, however that a greater efficiency can be achieved by shifting every other layer by 2.1 centimeters (half a golf ball). Assume that it will result in approximately 40% stacking efficiency (which can be illustrated by a simple drawing) – that is, instead of 70 layers of golf balls the pool will accommodate 98 layers (70 x 1.4). Therefore, the total amount of balls the swimming pool can accommodate is about 67.13 million (685,000 x 98).

o How many barbers are there in Chicago?

Chicago's population is close to 3 million → assume 50% are men → assume 6 haircuts per year → 9 million haircuts per year. Assume also that each haircut takes 30 minutes and the average barber works 8 hours a day, 5 days a week, 50 weeks a year (2 weeks vacation) → 4,000 haircuts per year. Therefore, there should be 2,250 barbers (assuming that all men get a haircut from a barber; if this is not the case, then the derived number is overestimated).

▸ Additional Estimation Questions:

o What is the weight of a Boeing 747?

o How many computers are sold daily?

o How many gas stations (pay phones, restaurants) are there in Chicago?

- How would you go about estimating your competitor's budget for advertising/promotional/R&D expenses?
- How many car batteries are sold in the United States each year?
- How many tennis balls can I fit in a football stadium?
- How many rotations does a tire on the front of a family sedan make on a road trip from New York to Boston?
- How many golf balls can fit in the typical suitcase?
- What is the maximum number of pencils I can fit across my desk without stacking them?
- Estimate the speed at which your fingernails grow in miles per hour.
- How much beer is consumed in Germany every year?
- What was the total volume added to landfills in the U.S. because of disposable diapers last year?
- How much tea is there in China?
- At any moment, how many pennies are inside a shopping mall?
- How many two-liter bottles of soda will be sold in the U.S. next year?
- Estimate the number of blades of grass in the average suburban lawn.
- How many hotel-sized bottles of shampoo are produced each year around the world?
- Estimate the number of people born in the world yesterday.
- How many times does the average Forbes 500 CEO hit the key "E" on a key-board during a day?
- Estimate the number of hairs on your head.
- How tall is this building?
- How long does it take for a light bulb to turn on?
- How much milk is produced in the U.S. each year?
- How many tomatoes does Heinz use in its production of ketchup in one year?
- During the course of a day, how many people walk into London's Heathrow air-port?

Logic Cases: Problems and Solutions

Logic cases are a form of brainteaser cases commonly given in interviews to test your ability to deal with abstract problems and to observe your problem-solving process.

o Why are manhole covers round?

A round cover cannot fall into a manhole, whereas square or rectangular ones can (e.g., if placed diagonally). Round manhole covers are also easier to be rolled down the street if necessary.

o Why do Coke cans have an indent at the bottom?

To control can expansion so that, in case of pressure, it does not bulge in the opposite direction or at the sides, which would not allow the can to stand up normally and would make it less visually appealing.

o You are in a room with three light switches. Each one controls one light bulb in the next room. Your goal is to figure out which switch controls which light bulb. You may flick only two switches and may enter into the light bulb room only once.

The key is to realize that a light bulb can also be tested by touch. Flick the first switch, wait for a few minutes, then turn it off and flick the second switch. Enter the light bulb room. The bulb that is on connects to the second switch. The warm light bulb is controlled by the first switch.

o Consider a set of cards, each one having a letter on one side and a number on the other side. You are given a subset of four cards as follows (the upper side): D-K-3-7. You have to test the following rule: If a card has a D on one side, it has a 3 on the other side. You must decide which cards need to be turned over to know whether this sample of cards is consistent with the rule.

The correct cards are D and 7 (although 90% of people pick D and 3). Seeing what is on the reverse of the 7 card can lead to disconfirming the rule if a D shows up (whereas seeing what is on the reverse of the 3 card cannot disconfirm the rule and is, hence, non-informative).[1]

o A bat and a ball cost $1.10 in total. The bat costs $1 more than the ball. How much does the ball cost?

The ball costs five cents (although most people think it is ten cents).[2]

▸ Additional Logic Questions:

o What is the angle between the minute hand and the hour hand at 12:45?

o You have a bucket of three different colored buttons. You are blindfolded and asked to pick up two buttons of the same color. What is the minimum number of buttons you must pick up before you can be sure that you have least two different colored buttons in your hand?

o A special kind of plant doubles in height every year for fifteen years. In what year was it half its maximum height?

o You want to boil an egg for four minutes, but you only have a two-minute and a six-minute hourglass timer. How can you use these two hourglass timers to boil the egg?

o You are a merchant trying to cross a river. In your possession are a coyote, a rabbit, and bucket of freshly picked tomatoes. You have a boat, but you can only take one item at a time to cross the river. The trouble is, the coyote wants to eat the rabbit, and the rabbit wants to eat the tomatoes. How can you get yourself and your merchandise across the river?

o Three men challenge each other to a "truel" (a three sided duel). The three men have varying levels of skill, and the worst gunman is asked to fire first, followed by the intermediate gunman, and finally the best gunman, after which they will continue in this order until there is only one man left standing. Where should the first shooter aim?

o If you are on a boat and you throw a wooden barrel overboard, does the level of water rise, sink, or stay the same?

o A spider is trapped in a slippery bucket. Every day he climbs 15 inches up but slips down 10 inches. The bucket is 25 inches tall. How long does it take for the spider to get out?

o How can you divide a round birthday cake into 8 equal pieces with only 3 straight slices of a knife?

o What is unique about the number 854917632?

o If you put a coin into a bottle and then insert a cork into the bottle's opening, how can you take the coin out without removing the cork or breaking the bottle?

Source

[1] Wason, P. C. (1960), "On the Failure to Eliminate Hypotheses in a Conceptual Task," *Quarterly Journal of Experimental Psychology*, 12, 129-140.

[2] Kahneman, Daniel (2003), "Maps of Bounded Rationality: Psychology for Behavioral Economics Dagger," *American Economic Review*, 93, 1449.

Core Skills Sought by Companies

Most companies look for the same set of attributes in job candidates: core skills (leadership, analytical skills, creativity, teamwork, communication skills, management skills, capacity to learn, and drive), knowledge (functional, industry, and global knowledge), and the overall fit with the company (personality fit, commitment to the company, and interest in the functional area). Even though they look for the same skill set, companies vary in the way they articulate these skills. Following is a sample of the key skills sought by companies in the three most popular recruiting areas: consulting, marketing, and finance.[1]

Concentration in Consulting

AT Kearney

o Perceptive

o Resourceful

o Achieving

o Teaming

Bain & Company

o Intelligence

o Integrity

o Passion

o Ambition

Booz Allen Hamilton

o Critical thinking and problem solving

o Creativity

o Quantitative analytics

o Conceptual analytics

o Business and personal leadership

- Interpersonal skills
- Intellect, knowledge, and insight
- Interest

DiamondCluster International

- Strong analytical and problem solving skills
- Ability to add value and influence change
- Ability to work effectively in a team environment
- Demonstrated initiative and leadership
- Strong written and verbal communication skills
- Creativity and resourcefulness
- Honesty and integrity
- Commitment and reliability
- Adaptability and flexibility

Grant Thornton

- Hard working
- Creative
- Passion for excellence
- Integrity
- Teamwork

Kurt Salmon Associates

- Integrity
- Drive to excel
- Strong analytical and communication skills
- Personal resilience
- Team players
- Commitment

L.E.K. Consulting

- Intelligence
- Honesty
- Hard work

- Integrity
- Teamwork
- Good humor

Marakon Associates

- Structured and logical thinking
- A creative and analytical approach to problem solving
- Empathy, maturity, and professionalism
- An understanding of the business issues confronting CEOs and general management
- Ability to work and communicate effectively with clients and colleagues at all levels
- Desire to achieve high standards both personally and professionally
- Common sense

Mars & Company

- Strong quantitative skills
- Energy
- Maturity
- Creativity
- Uncommon common sense
- A sense of humor

McKinsey & Company

- Problem solving
- Achieving
- Personal impact
- Leadership

Mercer Management Consulting

- The ability to structure problems logically
- The ability to develop innovative yet practical solutions
- The ability to work effectively as members of a team
- The ability to communicate clearly with both colleagues and clients

○ The ability to take initiative and leadership both internally and with clients

Monitor Group

○ Capabilities

○ Capacity to learn

○ Commitment

ZS Associates

○ Analytical and quantitative skills

○ Strategic thinking

○ Personal presence

○ Business acumen

○ Strong communication skills

○ Commitment

○ Collegiality

○ Creativity

Concentration in Marketing

American Express

○ Ability to develop winning strategies and drive results

○ Strong focus on customer and client service

○ Personal excellence

○ Ability to drive innovation and change

○ Ability to build important relationships

○ Ability to communicate effectively across diverse global teams

Clorox

○ Talent

○ Drive

○ Focus on results

○ Innovation

○ Team player

- Leadership
- Passion

Gillette

- Organizational excellence
- Achievement
- Integrity
- Collaboration

Microsoft

- Long-term approach
- Strategic thinking
- Passion for products and technology
- Customer focus
- Individual excellence
- Team spirit
- Interpersonal skills

PepsiCo

- Results orientation
- Commitment to excellence
- Willingness to learn
- Sense of excitement
- Ability to innovate
- Intelligence
- Dedication

Procter & Gamble

- Leadership
- Risk-taking
- Innovation
- Solutions
- Collaboration
- Mastery

SC Johnson

- Leadership
- High initiative
- Analytical ability
- Teamwork skills
- Creativity
- Innovation

Unilever

- Determination to win
- Business focus
- Intellectual skills
- People skills
- Integrity

Concentration in Finance

CitiGroup

- Integrity
- Excellence
- Respect
- Teamwork
- Ownership
- Leadership

Deutsche Bank

- Customer focus
- Teamwork
- Innovation
- Performance
- Trust
- Passion to perform

Fidelity Investments

o Understanding of the financial services industry

o Knowledge of accounting and financial principles

o Ability to work effectively with senior executives

o Strong analytical skills

o Excellent time management skills

o Ability to organize, prioritize, and multi-task

o Excellent project management and presentation skills

Goldman Sachs

o Passion for excellence

o Belief in the power of the group

o Integrity

o Trust

o Leadership

o Desire to be challenged

o Drive

Lehman Brothers

o Problem solving and analytic ability

o Leadership

o Initiative

o Team player

o Self confidence

o Assertiveness

o Maturity

o Ability to interact with others, persuade, and listen

o Recognition of own strengths and weaknesses

Morgan Stanley

o Energetic

o Creative

o Well-rounded

- Outgoing
- Self-motivated
- Ability to learn quickly
- Strong quantitative and analytical skills
- Desire to thrive in a dynamic, high-pressure environment

UBS Investment Bank
- Problem analysis
- Judgment and decision making
- Innovation
- Communication and impact
- Drive and commitment
- Teamwork
- Planning and organizing

Notes

---

[1] For up-to-date information about the recruitment processes, please obtain the necessary information directly from the company.

Printed in the United States
100804LV00002B/166-168/A